A Fresh Start Will Put You on Your Way

poems by

Andie Francis

Finishing Line Press
Georgetown, Kentucky

A Fresh Start Will Put You on Your Way

Publisher: Leah Huete de Maines
Editor: Christen Kincaid
Cover Art: Valyntina Grenier, *Big Out Rainbow*
Author Photo: Photo Belamour
Cover Design: Ander Monson

Order online: www.finishinglinepress.com
also available on amazon.com

Author inquiries and mail orders:
Finishing Line Press
P. O. Box 1626
Georgetown, Kentucky 40324
U. S. A.

Table of Contents

four

A Genesis

for Lawrence

not a soul believes my sob story
in something this tight and exquisite

—Jane Miller

one

When We've Run Out of Money and/or Whiskey

To keep warm, I pretend to push the dim stars around with my tongue. If mouths count as night sky, then the stars are brightening. I get a head start by naming them after the artificial light they will replace. When I get to LED, I picture a lectern, and then I realize how I miss the great orators of the past. My lover thinks you cannot miss what you have never known. Might they come back now and use similes and find us here waiting in our pajamas on the porch?

This Poem Is about a Folk Song

The song is about a train
called the Midnight Special,
brother. The lights on the train
are bright. The only wind
comes from its barreling.

Let's gather everything
we've bartered. The smokes,
neat in their boxes. We'll load
our pockets and bicker. No, you
ate the honey buns. Let's see

before the train's big haul.
I'll stand on your shoulders,
give me a boost. How much
do you know about this world
when things can't just be?

When a piece of paper
is enough to make you go blind?
Let her apron alone, let her
cry out back. Our troubles
are lousy birthmarks.

Brother, I've found
the everlasting light in this
breeze. Let it shine us bare.

Meeting a Tree during My Insomniac Phase

In the barracks
I have the sheet
pulled up to my chin.

Whoever said poems
don't exist, I am awake
because of one.

Closure is an untroubled lie.
I hike to a madrona instead,
whose limbs also peel

through the night.
Its red lends itself to names.
Mine is blood—

rocketed into vials.
Looking away
doesn't mean the mind

can do the same.
I have rolled my tights
off in the dark again.

There is nothing
to watch here
except waves parting rocks.

Fort, what are you
without a stockade?
And what am I

but anticipation,
cross-legged beneath this tree
that burns longer, hotter

than its counterparts.

This Poem Is Not about a Folk Song

My lover takes me to a stranger's barn.

Each weekend, my thumbs mill the passenger seat on the way out of town. Or, I push the car's cigarette lighter in and let

the coil go cold. With my lover, I am aware of thumbs. Notice that ladder on my waist there. Barn opens up to more barn.

Let's get in. If this is a Woody Guthrie song, I am dancing along. This is no folk song, or I am an unused napkin.

Or, I shape a napkin into a bird and place it on the dash. There's no handle when there's no door.

Yes, a tattoo is a type of bird, perhaps in flight, pulled by the sky in a deliberate circle. But tattoos are not buttons. Tattoos may be handles.

I make a cloud cover of my jeans. My button, an untrampleable mass of hay. My worry is whether I am liked.

Napkins are needed. My skin is a lighter on its way toward the barn. My lover's thumbs.

So Much

a redder seal
atop

my beached
dress

caught its clap-
threat

in a rookery
wheel.

Monsoon Season

See these sand-pack hands? Look how many more laughs I can trap. I am forbidden to invite anyone over from town, but I keep their lips close. Our feet pass through pollen.

We wade through toys. The gate makes us strangers. The gate says, postpone your hips. Gather coconuts as they occur.

I've found a way to split them. I bring them to my mattress. I press my teeth all the way in, reach the husk, and wait there.

That which is all mine. A clothesline weighted with dresses.

What stays?

Not even a flame. You, night, you are a mouth.

Boat upside down on the beach. A family asleep in their bed.

I have wet hair. I am wheezing.

When I've Run Out of Coffee and/or First-Person Plural

To stay awake, I pretend I am wearing lace under my pajamas. If eyes can undress the night sky, then the bedroom light has burned out. My neighbors push a mattress wrapped in plastic through their front door and down the hall. I let myself make their new bed in the dark. When I get to the fourth corner, I remember Woody Guthrie—how he said his eyes were cameras, and then I realize another person inhabits my lover's basement. My lover thinks you forget how good a song is until your lover sings it to you. Might he come around now and use the right kind of pronoun and find me here wearing lingerie on the porch?

When My Head Hangs Too Low

I head straight for the canyon's ledge. While waiting, I remember the real donkey, packless, how its ribs appeared unsafe.

In a mythic rendition, the sun and moon are sister and brother. I am the sister pulling shallow roots, and I say, see my tough side? And brother responds, no, I am too far away.

Why, there must be another real donkey to free up this scene. Notice that picture window in the cactus line right there.

Just as I am rescued by the myth, it changes. The sun and the moon are now lovers, and the moon is still covered in soot. There's really nothing he can do.

Purple and orange wring the sky, and I wish I were in my lover's basement instead because he has hung paper stars from the ceiling, and we listen to Woody Guthrie on repeat.

I keep my eyes on this belt buckle of a sun for as long as I can stand.

Daughter as Disguise

I am the daughter. I ask for help. I ask what makes
a face without my father's eyes? My mother's turn.
What makes a room without a chair to take a load
off? What makes a name if you never hear it right.
Right, I follow a corner until it leads to another.
If a daughter is forever, then what is a corner?
Mine leads to a dog yelping from its hard place.
I want to forever leave this cul-de-sac. I want to
never return. I want to stop being punished for
what I was taught. But door-slam? A belt snap
is a reason to say *stop. I can't take any more. I'm
sorry. I'm sorry. I said, I'm sorry.* Or something
like that. Daughter as disguise. You can hit me,
but you can't use your hand. Belt becomes arm
without hand. Arm aims for skin. There's no hand
to blame. The non-buckle side. I am wearing skin.
Surely it must be there.

two

The Careful Sneezer

You love me not. Other kids warn me
your eyes will pop out of their sockets
if you plug your nose. I need my eyes
to see where my red shoes are pointed.

The handkerchief's held with one hand,
the right, and clamped to my face
just below my eyes, pre-*achoo.*
My breath's suddenly held too, as if I must

prevent myself from leaving. Every sneeze
is a bouquet from the body. Mouth says,
I am sorry. Nose says, *Please forgive me.*
No, you. I will not. I am wearing white pants.

To anticipate a sneeze requires a keen
awareness of one's place and time.
You may get an itch, a tickle that tells you
everything is about to change. Maybe you love me.

Ahead, towards what will be the once-clean
river. Even the river is braced by the beaver.
Others tell me *you might break a rib.*
Needed to protect my flower-

petal heart. My breath? It is needed to blow
out candles. Red shoes are less careful than candles.
White pants, less careful than sneezes.
My heart, least careful of all.

Watching the Game from My Bed

Imagine falling; a long way
meant it was purposeful.

I left the hospital without
a name. I was a skunk

dangling from a fence, dreamed
up. *Before conception already,*

pass the ball. My first mistake?
Whittling a stick to a point

and my swoop-necked rage
opening like a pitcher plant.

Not on purpose, I whittled
straight through my thumb

knuckle. *Pass the ball,*
baby curls. The brain can't be

more trained than the heart.
Ultimately, a chemical brings

us back to beginning, and I
have more than once deprived

your lips from mine. *Pass*
the ball, a play for my next

hospital bed. To challenge
deprivation is to drink bleach,

to write a love poem, you must
meltdown. Don't think ice cream.

Daytime Responsible

And yet all I have to do
is respond to violence.

Instead, I polish the silverware. Eat plums
and leave the pits to stain the nightstand.

Sirens still the bedroom windows.

Let's do a sit-in for the soul.

Not all of us here will check
the heat of the doorknob first.

                    Hedge bets.

This is where we left ashes.

                    Incapacitate.

Sorry doesn't even begin to cut it.

I grind my teeth
when I am able to sleep.

Repaired again
with needle and thread.

I am what I was before the taxidermy.

Lift the fat
to stroke the stitching.

But how do the organs trundle in so much dark?

When My Cape Takes Hold of Nothing

Thieved air pocket
beneath my cape.

A liver, a tar
pit that entraps

me in its laugh
track. Nothing like

your farthest eyes
after a moon-length

clearing. How even
my ledger, how tallied

my tendons, but I can
not picture this dredger

any differently. It is the
victim who is saved

for living helplessly.
My legs are brewage.

Arms, one weathervane,
a reminder of your

many talents. A red string
tied to the highest point

from which to dangle
or respond. Each breast

can cease its pageantry,
as can the machine

you thought would
hearten this scene.

More Chance for Disappointment

Before leaving, my lover tells me we are like that field of lightning rods. In a twenty-minute version, he catches a strike to show me the future. It's about seven-thirty, and the sun is low enough that we are among mice. Several tourists have begun to point in our direction. We are glints on a horizontal plane before we become cabin talk. We are not overcome by today's electricity. We have yet to determine what kind of sublime we are meant to be. For rods that do not protect anything, we attract static very well. Why not try isolation? Okay, he occupies the far edge, and I, the near. Then, that's what we do.

What You Let

Snow up to my hips. I want cold, the sink of my boot before it flattens. Frozen lock and metal key. Nose. Boot-strike door. Sleeve.

Hang my wool socks over a chairback. My boots still by the door. I shiver. Tuck my legs into myself. My way to the stove.

Wakened by my hair. To leave without looking through a window. Aspens dipped in white.

New Year's, I run, feel my footing. Too drunk to worry of slipping. Cold, if you let it.

Snow-bank cursive.

At the clearing, that crow hops to the other side of the trunk, out of sight. It will come around again in the quiet.

See?

I Am Going to See a Mass of Cells

whenever they leave my body
nothing

another tight dress threaded with light
and a pair of small ears out there

in the latest future
I tell them
I can tuck these stones of loss in further

as in my life
wheelbarrows

as in I stop sign
take you disappointment

full and complete
for two months

maybe three

Less Chance for Disappointment

My lover writes on my bedroom window, *I want to be more supportive.* In an eighteen-minute version, he hands me a Coca-Cola just within reach. It's about four-thirty, late enough that several neighbors are shirtless and crows have begun to shake distant trees. We read about what's possible before wrecking the lawn. We are not overcome by today's bombings. We have yet to determine what kind of man or woman is running for president. For two people who sleep less, we hold phones and soda cans very well. Why not pitch horseshoes? Okay, he opens the garage door and finds the rusted set marked *ten dollars* next to a box marked *lace.* Then, that's what we do.

three

The Title of This Poem Is Brothers

A brother is dead for a decade. Ocotillo
stem on. All brothers must pass through
the family gate before they disappear.

Littlest cane, how might you brace
me for a life? Not that it is your job, and I
may become the porcupine's jaw. Eventually,

in June, your flowers will be too close to ruin
to resist. Biggest cane, how might
your spines keep me from trouble? The family

gate doesn't cry. It is a sketch. It can be made
into a bed, a raft. My lover is brother to no one.
Says he will never leave for good. A group

of crows who are brothers are still
called a murder. They sleep together
for a reason. I like the fire I am alone with—

the same way I like the sweater on the road;
its aimless arms, like the fire's, never flail.

When I Should Have Been Gone

Six neighborhood crows feed from a trashcan, and now my position on the couch is unwelcome.

One crow slings a takeout box onto my driveway for the others. Any friendly neighbor would run out in defense, flapping their arms

as if caught on fire. I am alone on Christmas, and no one asked me to be. It is snowing, and backyard rivers are swift. When we lose a frozen river,

we can only remember a passage we might have looked forward to. In a mythic rendition, when the river thaws, it becomes a road again. I am the sister still carrying in wood for the small fire, and I say, see what I am doing instead? And brother responds, no, I am too far away.

Crows did not make the river.

Why, there must be a raven to play a trick on this scene. I tell them apart by the calls they make. Notice the sound from the plastic bag contemplating the driveway.

Just as I am fooled by the myth, the crows remind me of an empty dancehall down the road. A crow in the snow

is my lover in the dark with one leg over the balcony.

What to do about crows besides turn the porch light off and remind them that they too are unsafe.

A Fresh Start Will Put You on Your Way

Where would an astronaut
park her spaceship?
Considering she has pushed
her bowling ball
in anticipation of its collision,
and life forms gather
to hear Jailhouse Rock,
the void is not completely
empty. She is suspended
with her back to an earth
that won't listen. Atoms,
she thinks, appear as light,
so no wonder Elvis is still alive.
We used the word *gun*
over and over until
it became *love.*
This field is easily traversed
because the sandwiches disappear
at each asteroid. For it is spring
in California, and the sun
is burning a woman's shoulders.
Perhaps when one begins
to barrel toward the planet,
she will think less important
things aloud; she will find
a parking meteor.

Where Have You Been

A truck is transporting a home. It's a wind tunnel as it passes, and I want to give in. I want to be swallowed by this linen closet suddenly planted on the back of a truck. What are you going to say about bedroom windows? It is easy to be swallowed. It's more difficult to be the next to die. There's no use in what you can't get into by yourself. By that, I mean a dress of any kind, black or white. By that I mean you can't find yourself somewhere. Hello, buttons just out of reach. Hello, damned clasp. Steering wheel. Brown lawn. Why didn't you ask where I'm going?

When My Cape Is No Match for a Curtain

Bottle washer, close to
removable in their

trap catch. Picture your
cape and a farthest floor

beneath you, that off
like shucking, like tree-

shaking, an aimed
lungful your cape,

and you are okay. Move
along. Everything to

clock-milk in America,
sloshed over an edge

to be sunk reappears behind
a curtain by the dozen.

Belong here in handed
newness along a coast

where seals bloody themselves
to mate, me and you against

the metronome. What if
there is no thing worth saving

in this fingertip life? No
bough, no wheel, no mud-

chickens, plum, no water,
face in a crowd, pigeons,

boulder, legs, sap,
no letter, no falling stars?

To Be Sober Is to Be Sober

At first, you will glance at a layer of pollen that flecks the patio yellow. Why does the yellow patio resemble

an ashtray, a receptacle to collect smallness and/or revenge? And why is the patio, the ashtray, shaped

like a lung, one of two ways to stay alive? Because it is hard to be someone when you are not killing at least half

of yourself. My lover, for one, drinks scotch until he lights a sparkler in the dark bedroom where I am asleep.

Pope Francis has only one lung. For the record, it was not his fault. When a lung is removed, the other expands

to compensate for the extra space. Like the Pope's lone lung, like my lover's lit sparkler, you too, will have

to accept where you find yourself. Here, what is around except a hammock tied between a pair of honorable

pines? A hammock. Two trees. It can be this easy. But if trees are harmless, you will be lost. I mean it will take a while to believe

in harmlessness, in things as they are. In van Gogh's painting, *Starry Night,* he did not paint the *iron-barred window* of his studio.

Imagine the purple swirls, the yellow and white spiraled stars of the painting. Now, the real skyline, boxy and behind bars.

In the hammock, there is nothing to censor. Sober, you will think: my mind and body are being reclassified by this hammock's

swinging. Hello, lover who is dangerous. Hello, friend behind bars. Pollen in my hair. This wrist can later be used to launch a pinecone or a lighter. I can direct my lover's hand in the dark. These thighs can disrupt a stash of pine needles or

stomp a glass bottle. Thighs can memorize the shape of my lover's ears—each proof that I am still alive. For the record, van Gogh's self-

mutilation is a myth. It was his friend, Gauguin, who cut van Gogh's ear during a sword fight.

Yes, and in the hammock, it is all over, over, and you will be okay, and you will be okay.

Someone is Watching the Microphone

backyard Airstream
wears the glint of morning—

a bathrobe reminds me
I am an act, a lip-sync

human with enough
hairbrush, more

all ya gotta do's
to convince the day

I won't need a guardrail.
I will not be your bucket

of pulp today with each
angled glance in the mirror.

Eyebrows sing *hug me,*
squeeze me. Cheeks can

play more homemaker than
wrecker. It is myth that lets

us forget our own creature.
So what if I am the cause

of a dirtied flag? An empty
propane tank I'd better

explain. I, too, am here
to get my soul

known again, to see how far
rear-views will take me.

How It Begins

Pillows keep my head from the wall,
or else my hand. Blood,
a neighbor's buzzsaw. Three crows perched on a wire.
  Wire.
Use my fingers,
   water, to desoil.

   If I look I will be sick.
As if my arm is not pinned beneath us.

   What makes you think of crying?
   A linen closet? Piecing a dinner plate? Once my thighs in
   the mirror.
Wait to finish.

   Lace the corners.
   A chapel, or rather a steeple
   at the end. You knew me
   never.

   The doused part,
see the bed
I haven't made.
Mattress in on itself.

   Hallow?
How to disguise me.

This is supposed to be fun.
   Hiddenly so.

Why don't you   anymore?

At the bathroom sink
thinking I ought to be.

I am trying to say will you
give me up.

          For sake, I will   myself.
The sheets will dry.

I'm thinking of my mother.
          Bell bottoms she used to wear.
          An ocotillo that was just bare.

I'm cleaning my face.
This is me, clean-faced.

four

A Genesis

7. An Enter for Rest

Now rest
who finish
a good breath's rest.
Breathing to allow an enter for rest.
In
to set our position at rest,
comfortable to lay the calm to rest,
rest us
cotton at rest,
a pearl rest,
to let a bright light rest.
Whole   out,
our essence rested on the table
to let ripple-less rest.
The wreath rests within
us rest.
A light rests upon the altar
to rest our self
who make
rest now.
Raised up in   out
to rest our wing against a tree,
to rest our eyes on the body,
rest our face.
The rest of the place is us;
all the rest are lumens.
Long breath in
will rest assure   out
who create
rest
now.

6. *Pump Blood into Day*

Staying inside here.
For strange kinds. Creeping things. For beasts. Take stock now.
        at the present time or moment: *she is here now*
Screech and scurry where once still
except wind. Field cycle.
Pump blood into day. Watch everything that creeps
breathe. Size lungs. Elasticity
the tissues have. Watch how differently they pant.
After slithering, narrow the rib cage. Widen
to grip. Howl wares. Splash components. Rustle limbs.
Snag coating. Mouths learn, watch them hinge now.
        (more emphatically) immediately
or at once: *now or never*
Huge gallop muscles. Later, wear
scrub into way. Heel snort. Heel flare.

How much space does the heart occupy?

Back before dusk saying, multiply. Good
and green there, every fruit very good
and ready. Now,
at this time or juncture in some period
under consideration or in some course
of proceedings described: *the case now passes to the jury*

let us make
likeness. Our image.

Let us hold out these arms we made now
        at the time or moment only just past.

5. Distractions, Circular as Time

Pummel this morning, even closer to start, simply consider depth.
Use it to measure abundance. Measure such feeling or thought.
May sink or fall. May heighten. Rise.

Did you spill gasoline
and try to hide?

Where you can, exquisite waters bring forth your kind.
Whale, become. You radiant whale, moveth
below. Lung bellow. Look at the blow, then gusher.
      in or to a lower place; lower down; beneath
Multiply your blubber. Make up with enough ply.
Others, unhinge your nuptial pincers.
Hope to carry another until she hardens.
Current passes over gills. Fish teem below.
      at a later point on a page
      or in writing: *see the statistics below*

Living: heavens, you are not without.
Here also begins earth movement.
May fly. May wings. Fowl. May winged birds flap.
Flap in praise. Fly above, may fly, fly above
      in or to a higher place; overhead: *the blue sky above*
Swarm. Fill sky with v.
      a consonant, the 22nd letter of the English alphabet

Distractions, circular as time.
Good idea to fill in everything beak
and feather. Pluck. Separate. Molt.
Feather expanse. Open close in the open.
Talon above, let you fly birds, let you succeed now.
      before in order, especially in a book
      of writing: *from what has been said above*
Saying, multiply.

4. And Great Lights Light

And great lights give. And great lights light. And great lights light upon.
        up and on; upward so as to get or be on
Let them. Let them two great lights of the heavens
arrive and remain. Expanse full. Greater light. Sun.
Star and stars. Look up, rays push outward.
Backbone.
Direct heat downward ray,
out of our heavens' golden hold.
Lightwave crest. Light boulder. Heat
bark. Heat orchards. Wrought. Slice hillsides.
Shadow bauble. Dark mound. Jagged victory
directly overhead.

What are the seven
spikes on the crown?

Sweet sun, too, is wintering air, masses of snow and ice.
Smatter earth's shoulders white. Accompany cold
days, finite, with ruled folds.
Spring, at attention. And sun-upon.
        in an elevated position on

Sprung-upon. Summer.
Compare infinite stars. So. So. So. So. So.
Yes, just the ticket. Ticketed. Ticketed.
Morning penned to day:
It is the east, and so, is the sun.

See how her shadow seems
longer in the evening?

Tick day from night. Day night. Fall back. Day, night.
Another great but lesser light
rule. It is the moon with its lips
upon earth's shoulders.

on, in any of various senses
(as an equivalent of on with no
added idea of ascent or elevation)
Beam dune. Beam savanna. Beam paddles.
Beam canopy. Swallow milkweed. Glint swallow.

And the broken
chains?

Medium as much as message.
How I am sense-making. See good
light blast even further. Years.
Here, hold out for more.

3. Because Everything Is Unruly

Come, come Seas. One, two. Three. Four,
five, and six. Seven. Bless river. Come lake. Bless stream. Spray. Sud
this way. Sud-sud. Sud-sud. Scullery-steam I am.
Come rain. Bless rain. Yes, bless rain
pools of light, pool-emphasis, pools to lift the hand to lift the hem,
lift back pull, got *l*, want puddles of *q*, soak,
I think I understand, keep an eye out,
ice, it's that it must be frozen.
Move further, further apart you
          in pieces, or to pieces: *to take a watch apart*
Use the blue again, needle, left to right, left to right, left
right, clothe the whole,

The color of the tongue
tells us if we are sick?

Now scour toward. Different than *to* because
          also towards
          in the direction of (with reference to either motion or position): *to walk*
          toward the north

To pluck towards, too. Scrub towards, swill
toward homophonic. Beautiful nuisances.
Yes, said it, down, down to drool.

Why, I cry to hear
myself, didn't you?

Scale, once the gathering begins, still want *q*
          a consonant, the 17th letter of the English alphabet
Come clouds, yes,
clouds, just glub this part,
activate the agape, activate
          to make active.
          in a state of action; in actual progress or motion: *active hostilities*

process or state of acting or of being active: *the machine is not now in*
action
serving temporarily; substitute: *acting governor*
to act as a servant
a person employed in domestic duties
Down, down, to the essential, scuff,
always that which is outside,

all bets, dry land.
Bet the earth sprouts. Bet the low dwelling
grasses, more than grass because everything is unruly.
Bet ferns. Take root. Take green. Forest plants are yielding, yield seeds, yield
moss, groves of lemon trees, blame the fruit in which is their seed,
each according to its pucker, apple to its bite, orange to its bitter, grapes, give
them flesh,
olive pit, no, not for peace yet, on and on forth the *Earth*

But whose park
bench is this?

2. A Series of Separations

Good, greater light again, and now for a series of separations.
Lift, lift as high as possible, and then slowly release
waters from the waters
        with a specifying or particularizing effect, as opposed
        to the indefinite or generalizing force of the indefinite: *I liked the book*
        that you gave to me
Try to plash the firmament because it is durable. Yes, apply pressure
until it's poised.
Float beneath and hold five breaths—sapphire, indigo, powder,
powder, how does color appear?

Did the snake die inside its coil?

Flung to the other side above the canopy.
The vault is so.
        (See be)
        to exist; have reality; live; take place; occur; remain as before: *she is no*
        more,
        it was not to be, think what might have been

The world at this time
could not disrupt sound. Strike at the center
when trying to reduce, to order. As in jaw seize, as in larrup
until all turns blue.

Why is the sky so blue when asking for a favor?

Hhhhhh
Heaven.
Heavening
  evening.
More ring.
Morning.

1. Several Strings Stretched Over or Under

First things first. Heavens,
Earth. Earth-jut. Not just jutting,
but also out, because at this time rules applied to rugged mass.
        to extend beyond the main body or line; project; protrude (often
        followed by *out*)
Jutted out, original colors—rust, copper, ecru—
once submerged, not in water but emptiness,
now become shades.

What if gum was stuck
beneath the table all along?

Okay, heavens. Can be cavernous,
into, for light only returns
longitudinally. Have *Day* to depend on.
        in to; in
        expressing motion or direction toward the inner
        part of a place or thing, and hence
        entrance or inclusion within limits, or change
        to new circumstances, relations, conditions, forms, etc.

Hence, if sound existed already. As shelter. In hieroglyph.
Several strings stretched over, or under,
and up to create vibration. Articulate
human, but not yet.

Still, listen
stiff, a darkness between, *Night*, belly, listen like this
slower than out
        and to
        serving to specify a point
        approached and reached: *come to the house*

What's noisy about

a syringe in the gutter?

The sounds? Burial. Blotted to bury.
Dig to press oil, remember
how to write with water.
In and to existence.

Notes

"This Poem Is about a Folk Song" references lyrics from the song "Midnight Special."

"So Much" is after William Carlos Williams's "The Red Wheelbarrow."

"The Careful Sneezer" is after Harvey Lomaheftewa's 1941 painting *The Careful Sneezer.*

"Watching the Game from My Bed" was written in collaboration with David Thacker in response to Terrance Hayes's ars poetica prompt.

"When My Cape Takes Hold of Nothing" references images from several poems: Amy Lowell's "Pyrotechnics;" Ezra Pound's "In a Station of the Metro" and "A Girl;" and William Carlos Williams's "The Red Wheelbarrow" and "This Is Just To Say."

"A Fresh Start Will Put You on Your Way" references a joke in the first and last lines of the poem; the title relies on a fortune cookie.

"Where Have You Been" references the title of Joyce Carol Oates's "Where Are You Going, Where Have You Been?"

"To Be Sober Is to Be Sober" references *The Letters of Vincent van Gogh.*

"How It Begins" is after Carolyn Forché's "Sequestered Writing."

"A Genesis" was adapted from Genesis 1:1-1:31 in the English Standard Version of the Holy Bible and includes definitions from *The American College Dictionary.*

"Because Everything Is Unruly" uses "beautiful nuisances" in reference to François Dufrêne's sound poem, "Belles nuisances, hantez nos nuits."

Acknowledgments

Thank you to the editors and staffs of the following journals, in which these poems, a few in different forms, first appeared:

Berkeley Poetry Review: "Monsoon Season" and "This Poem Is Not about a Folk Song"

Cathexis Northwest: "Someone Is Watching the Microphone"

Cimarron Review: "How It Begins" and "Daytime Responsible"

Columbia Poetry Review: "I Am Going to See a Mass of Cells" and "So Much"

CutBank: "What You Let"

The Greensboro Review: "When My Head Hangs Too Low"

Harpur Palate: "Daughter as Disguise"

The Lindenwood Review: "Less Chance for Disappointment" and "More Chance for Disappointment"

The Penn Review: "When I've Run Out of Coffee and/or First Person Plural"

Portland Review: "A Fresh Start Will Put You on Your Way"

Prick of the Spindle: "This Poem Is about a Folk Song"

TAMMY: "To Be Sober Is to Be Sober"

Timber Journal: "Meeting a Tree During My Insomniac Phase"

Willow Springs: "When We've Run Out of Money and/or Whiskey"

Zone 3: "The Title of This Poem Is Brothers"

Thanks to *The Greensboro Review* and *Cimarron Review,* respectively, for allowing "When My Head Hangs Too Low" and "Daytime Responsible" to be reprinted by Four Chambers Press for *The Narrow Chimney Reader.*

Thanks to the editors and readers with the University of Akron Press, [PANK] Books, Zone 3 Press, and Ghost Peach Press, all of whom selected this manuscript as a finalist or semifinalist. Thanks to the editors of *Harpur Palate* for nominating "Daughter as Disguise" for a Pushcart Prize (2021), the editors of *The Penn Review* for nominating "When I've Run Out of Coffee and/or First-Person Plural" for Best New Poets (2020), and the editors of *The Lindenwood Review* for nominating "Less Chance for Disappointment" and "More Chance for Disappointment" for Best of the Net (2019). Thanks to the editors of CutBank for naming "What You Let" as a finalist for the Patricia Goedicke Prize in Poetry (2012) and for giving me my first publication with that poem.

/ /

My gratitude to Jane Miller, Ander Monson, Joshua Marie Wilkinson, Chris Cokinos, Alison Hawthorne Deming, Aurelie Sheehan, Annie Guthrie, John Melillo, Terrance Hayes, Shane McCrae, and Dora Malech for their teaching and counsel, both short and long, and in unexpected ways.

My appreciation to Valyntina Grenier for allowing me to adopt her visual art for the cover, and to Ander for his cover design.

My continuing gratitude to Christen Kincaid, Leah Huete de Maines, and the rest of the team at Finishing Line Press, for seeing enough potential in this book to bring it into the world.

Thanks to Meg Wade, Hannah Ensor, Jeevan Narney, Ben Rutherfurd, Jordan Young, Jamison Crabtree, Megan Coe, and Will Cordeiro for their insight and close readings of these poems in various stages.

Thanks, also, to my friends Lindsay and Jeff MacMaster, Gina Neller, Erin Dendorfer, Billy Ostroff, Heather and Luke Cameron, Beth Barnes, Sarah Minor, Tommy Mira y Lopez, Angie Hansen, Nicole Walker, Erik Sather, Jess Martini, Amanda Meeks, Stacy Murison, and Kim Hensley Owens. And, thanks to Justin Barnes, my brother from another mother, for inspiring me to commit to a life of making art, just as you have.

Thanks to my family, the Francises and Sweets, the Lenharts, and the Slapniks, and especially to my parents and brother. Mom, this would not have been possible without your confident release of me into the wild. Dad, you are the one that instilled in me the art of storytelling. Mike, thanks for always sharing your love for music and poetry with me. Kristen, Ford, and Shepard, the river poems are for you. Larry and Marilyn, you've reminded me that it always gets better. And Pixel and Josie—you remain my trusted editors-in-chief.

To Lawrence, my lover, for whom I wouldn't have a book or a future without— thanks for choosing to hang in this hammock with me.

And Milo and Greta, you are the great lights.

And God, thank you for giving me the courage and space to make my art, especially when it feels impossible.

Andie Francis is the author of *I Am Trying to Show You My Matchbook Collection* (CutBank Books, 2014) and *A Fresh Start Will Put You on Your Way* (Finishing Line Press, 2022). She is Poetry Editor for *Carbon Copy* and an assistant poetry editor for *DIAGRAM*. Her work has appeared in *Berkeley Poetry Review, Cimarron Review, Columbia Poetry Review, Greensboro Review, Harpur Palate,* and elsewhere. She holds a BA in English from the University of East Anglia and an MFA in poetry from the University of Arizona. Francis has taught writing at Northern Arizona University, the University of Arizona, and in the San Francisco, Sacramento, and Folsom Cordova Unified School Districts. She currently lives in Flagstaff, Arizona.

www.ingramcontent.com/pod-product-compliance
Lightning Source LLC
Chambersburg PA
CBHW021204090426
42740CB00008B/1227